# GOLDEN GLOWS FROM PLATINUM SKY

## MORNINGS AND SUMMERS

## HIDDEN DEMOISELLE

THIS BOOK IS DEDICATED TO EVERYONE.

# Contents


*Foreword*                                    *xi*

*Preface*                                     *xiii*

*Acknowledgements*                            *xv*

*Prologue*                                     *xvii*

1. Words                                       1

2. Relate                                      2

3. Morning                                     3

4. Darkness                                    4

5. Softness                                    5

6. Thoughts                                    6

7. Colours                                     7

8. Five                                        8

9. Heavy                                       9

10. Dream                                      10

11. Beginning                                  11

12. Grey                                       12

13. Eyes                                       13

14. Leave                                      14

15. Bloom                                      15

16. Struggle                                   16

17. Bird                                       17

18. Pleasure                                   18

19. Awake                                      19

20. Water                                      20

# Contents


21. Unknown     21

22. Dawn     22

23. Minute     23

24. White     24

25. Black     25

26. Mistake     26

27. Warm     27

28. Crowd     28

29. Life     29

30. Pyjama     30

31. Plans     31

32. Lose     32

33. Brave     33

34. Curtain     34

35. Bread & Butter     35

36. Day     36

37. Yellow     37

38. Count     38

39. Say     39

40. Introverts     40

41. Weekend     41

42. Carry     42

43. Out     43

44. Heart     44

# Contents


45. Slow     45

46. Light     46

47. Care     47

48. Longing     48

49. Noon     49

50. Courage     50

51. Bone     51

52. Small     52

53. Change     53

54. Afternoon     54

55. Flowers     55

56. Imagine     56

57. Hot     57

58. Rustling     58

59. Lost     59

60. Sun     60

61. Star     61

62. Step     62

63. Weapon     63

64. Mutual     64

65. Tea     65

66. Run     66

67. World     67

68. Velvet     68

# Contents


69. Unseen — 69

70. Blue — 70

71. Thaw — 71

72. Home — 72

73. Meaning — 73

74. Coolness — 74

75. Frozen — 75

76. Blur — 76

77. Traffic — 77

78. Chapter 78 — 78

79. Sweet — 79

80. Compliment — 80

81. Melt — 81

82. Dilly-dally — 82

83. Drip — 83

84. Cloudy — 84

85. Up — 85

86. Thirst — 86

87. Long — 87

88. Time — 88

89. Breath — 89

90. Burn — 90

91. Walk — 91

92. Same — 92

# Contents


| | |
|---|---|
| 93. Exhaustion | 93 |
| 94. Shower | 94 |
| 95. Ice-cream | 95 |
| 96. Smart | 96 |
| 97. Blankets | 97 |
| 98. Sweater | 98 |
| 99. Nature | 99 |
| 100. Stone | 100 |
| 101. Indifferent | 101 |
| 102. Shrewd | 102 |
| 103. Cowards | 103 |
| 104. Middle | 104 |
| 105. Truth | 105 |
| 106. Difference | 106 |
| 107. Late Afternoon | 107 |
| 108. Growth | 108 |
| 109. Trees | 109 |
| 110. Soon | 110 |
| 111. Violet | 111 |
| 112. Warning | 112 |
| 113. Everything | 113 |
| 114. Sand | 114 |
| 115. Storm | 115 |
| 116. Way | 116 |

# Contents


117. Aroma 117

118. Evening 118

Greatful 119

# Foreword

It's a moment of joy and absolute admiration to announce the second book, **"Golden Glows From Platinum Sky"** written by my daughter, Alshifa, at such a young age.

Her noble ideas, peculiar perspectives and ingenious thought process totally baffles me in a proud way. Once she finds meaning in something trivial, the matter no longer remains trivial.

This book is an absolute masterpiece. It correlates various aspects of nature with our lives. *Reading, Listening or even trying to Fathom* each and every quote relishes a soothing effect which I'm sure shall linger for long within each one's mind.

I'm hopeful that this book shall be read and appreciated by all the readers and writers out there.

AZIM LAIQUE KHAN

# Preface

*The tranquil feeling of dawn, morning dimness and its eventually brightening light; the analgesic feeling of slumber and its warmth; the cheerfulness felt when long walks turn into fantasy and this whole world seems rhythmic; the feeling of provocation under the scorching sun;* for quite sometime now, my mind has been flushed by such variegated feelings.

In my heart, I knew there's nothing better than to give my feelings words, adore them with well framed sentences and reveal them to the whole world as quotes.

And this book here is just that.

I hope you fathom and relate with me. I would love nothing more.

# Acknowledgements

I want to express my deepest gratituse towards my parents, **Azim & Aliya Khan**, who have always supported me with my talent, my art, my projects, my tantrums and assisted me in decision making, many dilemmas and always made me feel motivated.

And my brother, **Mohammed**.

I also want to express my heartfelt gratitude towards my friend, *Savedna*, who is my very first fan and has always been supportive and encouraging.

And most of all, I'm greatful for the mind-blowing and wonderful life I have been given by God.

# Prologue

**"GOLDEN GLOWS FROM PLATINUM SKY"** is a book that

describes the

white mornings and silver summer sky through which the

gleaming

golden and intense rays scatter sleekly over this whole world,

sowing various emotions and

painting variegated colours which depicts mutualism amongst

people.

Each one feels the summer, each one feels the heat, each one

reacts the same.

Every human is connected in one or other way.

I hope golden rays surge from our platinum hearts as well.

# 1. WORDS

*EVERY WORD DEMANDS TO BE UNDERSTOOD.*

*Some things only take a second*

*to be read but all life to*

*be understood.*

# 2. RELATE

*RELATIONS OTHER THAN BLOOD MATTER.*

*All I ever want is to be related*

*to each one with the*

*words I say.*

# 3. MORNING

*Half awake, half unawake;*

*Half aware, half unaware;*

*A ray of sunlight,*

*A stroke of dim light*

*—Morning barges in.*

# 4. DARKNESS

**SOMETIMES, UGLY IS BEAUTIFUL.**

*Morning is different.*

*It's one of those few moments when*

*darkness feels comforting*

*and light hurts.*

# 5. SOFTNESS

Soft touch of blanket on our skin;

Soft gushing air through our hair;

We're brave enough to let go of such softness.

# 6. THOUGHTS

**THINKING COSTS BRAIN.**

*Not yet awake and here our*

*thoughts plunder*

*away our*

*brain.*

# 7. COLOURS

*Orange summer light,*

*Early yellow sky,*

*But hearts still remain grey*

*in pursuit of colours.*

# 8. FIVE

*"No problem," I mumbled.*

*"Just five more minutes..." I mumbled again.*

# 9. HEAVY

## HEAVINESS BRINGS SLUMBER.


*Heavy heart. Heavy mind. Heavy eyelids.*


*Feel. Think. Sleep.*

# 10. DREAM

**FEW THINGS NEVER LEAVE US.**

*Sleep and forget.*

*Dream and remember.*

# 11. BEGINNING

*THERE'S ALWAYS A WAY TO BEGIN.*

*The shifting sound of drawing the*

*curtains away marks the*

*beginning of*

*morning.*

# 12. GREY

*COLOURS SPEAK.*


*Mornings are grey—dim and bright.*

# 13. EYES

*MOST THINGS ARE DONE JUST TO GET
UNDONE.*

*Open your eyes just so you can squint them.*

# 14. LEAVE

## *HOLD ON TO THINGS THAT ARE YET TO COME.*

*Leave behind things that can't hold on to you.*

*Leave behind the yesterdays.*

*Leave behind the last night.*

# 15. BLOOM

*EVENTUALLY, EVERYTHING BLOOMS.*


*A flower will bloom with the rising sun.*


*A person might bloom with*


*each passing day.*

# 16. STRUGGLE

**STRUGGLE IS UNDEFINED.**

*Struggle is not staying awake all night.*

*It's actually sleeping at 5*

*and waking at 8.*

# 17. BIRD

*WE OFTEN WISH TO BE WHAT WE'RE NOT.*


*Don't you sometimes wish to become*


*a chirping bird, merry in its*


*own small world?*

# 18. PLEASURE

## TO KNOW WHAT PLEASURE IS, IS A PLEASURE.

*Pleasure is a cup of strong tea in bed!*

# 19. AWAKE

*A FACE IS NEVER TRUSTWORTHY ENOUGH.*

*I wore the face the world knows,*

*I rose from the grave of slumber I slept in—*

*I woke up.*

# 20. WATER

*Sleep is just like a closed knob of a tap.*

*As soon as you wake up the knob twists,*

*and all the lost thoughts gush in like water.*

# 21. UNKNOWN

*UNKNOWN, EVERYTHING IS.*

*Unknown—the day ahead.*

*Unknown—the life beyond.*

# 22. DAWN

## *TIME TO SLEEP AND TIME TO WORK ARE ONE.*

*Some know the peacefulness of dawn.*

*While others know it's rush!*

# 23. MINUTE

*THE TIME GIVEN TO YOURSELF IS NEVER WASTE.*

*Secure the second, don't let it pass away.*

*But if you wish to give yourself a little more time—*

*Just hold on for a minute!*

# 24. WHITE

**_WHITE THINGS ARE PRETTY._**

_White windows,_

_Brown chairs,_

_White skin,_

_Brown hair._

# 25. BLACK

*BLACK THINGS ARE BEAUTIFUL.*

*Black curtains,*

*Black chair,*

*Black skin,*

*Black hair.*

# 26. MISTAKE

*PAST DEMANDS TO BE REMEMBERED.*

*No one really cares about the mistake*

*you made after you make*

*another mistake.*

# 27. WARM

*LET YOURSELF FEEL GOOD THINGS.*

*Let your skin feel warm from the water.*

*Let your heart feel warm from your breath.*

# 28. CROWD

**CROWD IS ESSENTIAL.**

*No one thinks straight with eyes closed,*

*door locked and the world away.*

*One thinks straight amidst the crowd.*

# 29. LIFE

## *CROWD IS ESSENTIAL YET AGAIN.*

*Life is crowded—*

*On the streets.*

*In the minds.*

# 30. PYJAMA

*FIND YOUR TREASURE.*

*Pyjamas and all the other things which*

*aren't hard on us are treasures.*

# 31. PLANS

*NOT VERY GREAT MINDS NEED TO PLAN.*

*Great things happened when great minds*

*had nothing planned for the day.*

# 32. LOSE

**OVERNIGHT, THINGS CHANGE.**

*We lose ourselves piece by piece till*

*we're completely lost by the night.*

*Next morning we're found again.*

# 33. BRAVE

## *CHOSING COMFORT IS UNEASY.*

*Not everyone are brave enough to choose*

*comfort over a pretty uneasy dress.*

# 34. CURTAIN

***LIGHT THINGS CAN'T STOP BRIGHT THINGS.***

*You need a little darkness.*

*Plain white curtains can never*

*stop the piercing rays.*

# 35. BREAD & BUTTER

*WE HAVE NO IDEA ABOUT THINGS CLOSE TO US.*

Bread and butter will always remain close to my heart.

And tea, close to my brain.

# 36. DAY

**WE LOSE IT WHILE THINKING.**

*As the day passes, I think about how will the day pass!*

# 37. YELLOW

*SUMMER SHADES BURN.*

*Black. Violet. Blue. Orange. Yellow.*

*More yellow.*

*Burning hot yellow.*

# 38. COUNT

*WE FAIL THE MOMENT WE START COUNTING.*

*Don't keep counts like how we never count*

*the number of times we've looked*

*in the mirror.*

# 39. SAY

*MOST TIMES WE DON'T KNOW WHAT TO SAY.*

*Say, "okay."*

*Say, "fine."*

*You don't have to mean it. Just say.*

# 40. INTROVERTS

**_INTROVERTS HAVE POWER._**

_Introverts are blessed with the quirk to become_

_invisible whenever they want._

# 41. WEEKEND

*NOT EVERYTHING THAT MELTS IS CHOCOLATE.*


*Weekends are chocolates;*


*For melting away.*

# 42. CARRY

*CARRYING FRAGILE THINGS IS AN ART.*

*Don't wait for the breeze to carry you.*


*Carry yourself away.*

# 43. OUT

*FRESH AIR IS THE BEST REMEDY.*

*When you don't know, just go out.*

*When you know more, just go out.*

# 44. HEART

**THINGS CHANGE.**

*Even the coldest hearts become wax in summer.*

# 45. SLOW

*YOU ARE NOT THE ONE LACKING.*


*Your mind isn't slow, the world's faster.*


*The fan isn't slow, the heat is stronger.*

# 46. LIGHT

**_EVERYTHING IS MORE AND LESS._**

_They told you to find the light._

_They never told you to find the light that warms,
not burns._

# 47. CARE

*YOU WON'T HAVE TO DEAL WITH IT IF YOU DON'T CARE.*

*Everything becomes cool once you stop caring.*

*Like summer.*

# 48. LONGING

*SOMETIMES WE LONG JUST FOR LITTLE.*

*Usually we long for things that are not there.*

*In summer, we long for warmth when*

*there's heat everywhere.*

# 49. NOON

*THERE'S NO STOPPING.*

Nothing can detain one's longing to breathe fresh air.

Not even scorching noon.

# 50. COURAGE

*IF WE WANT, WE DO.*


*The heat shall burn me,*


*but I'll still find the courage to walk under it.*

# 51. BONE

*YOU DON'T NEED A CLOCK ALWAYS.*

*You know it's 12 when the rays*

*pierce you till your bones.*

# 52. SMALL

**WE'RE SMALL AND BIG AT THE SAME TIME.**

*We're so small in this world and yet*

*a big part of this society.*

# 53. CHANGE

*NOTHING CAN CHANGE US.*


*It's strange no fire, no heat, absolutely nothing*


*can stop people or change their mind.*

# 54. AFTERNOON

**DIFFICULT TIME ALWAYS PASSES.**

*Afternoon is the most difficult time to pass.*

# 55. FLOWERS

## *ONE THING BENEFITS AND DOESN'T.*

*Some flowers die and fall,*

*some flowers bloom and sway;*

*Under the sunlight.*

# 56. IMAGINE

## *SEE THE WORLD UNDER SHADE.*

*Sun blazing everywhere and clouds shading upon us.*

*Imagine!*

# 57. HOT

*NOT UNDERSTANDING CREATS A MESS.*

*I might say, "so damn hot," between our conversations.*

*Just know, it's not about you.*

# 58. RUSTLING

## WEAKER AND WEAKER, CENTURY BY CENTURY.

*The trees rustled about how they survived*

*decades of summer to people*

*who couldn't last*

*a day.*

# 59. LOST

**BEING LOST IS LOSING.**

*Nothing matters when you're lost in the surrounding.*

*Nothing makes sense when you're lost in yourself.*

# 60. SUN

**COMPETE WITH BETTER THINGS.**


*Only a cup of hot tea might stand a chance*


*against a sheath of hot sun.*

# 61. STAR

*PEOPLE ARE NOT WHAT THEY SEEM.*

*People are stars.*

*They sometimes start burning like the sun.*

# 62. STEP

## *SHOW YOURSELF WHAT EEDS TO BE SHOWN.*

*I step out to show myself the*

*pleasures of stepping in.*

# 63. WEAPON

*NO ONE IS BARE HANDED.*


*We're scared of weapons when*


*each one carries words.*

# 64. MUTUAL

*MUTUALISM IS RARE.*

*People start caring less mutually in summer*

*because each one bears the stench*

*of sweat and bars of anger.*

# 65. TEA

*TEA OUTRANKS.*


*Lemonade? No tea!*


*Coffee? No tea!*

# 66. RUN

**YOU KNOW WHERE TO RUN TO.**

*Run after the light and burn yourself.*

*Run after the shade and warm yourself.*

# 67. WORLD

### *THE WORLD IS UNKNOWN.*

Three worlds I know of—

The world outside.

The world inside.

The world within.

# 68. VELVET

**TEACH YOURSELF.**

*Liberating yourself of the velvet might help*

*you learn how to handle silk!*

# 69. UNSEEN

*FEELINGS ARE REAL.*

*When it's noon, we can't find stars*

*but we definitely can feel it.*

# 70. BLUE

**BRIGHT DOESN'T ALWAYS MEAN RIGHT.**

*Even some bright days can be blue and grey.*

# 71. THAW

## *HARSHNESS CAN THAW PEOPLE'S HEARTS.*

*Where people can't, summer can—thaw.*

# 72. HOME

**TO THINK TO UNTHINK.**

*I think of taking a walk just to*

*think of coming home again.*

# 73. MEANING

*How satisfyingly can summer suggest*

*both agitation and soberness!*

# 74. COOLNESS

**SUMMER TEACHES BEST LESSONS.**

*Walk amidst the heat waves to realize*

*the warmth of coolness.*

# 75. FROZEN

*ICE CAN BURN.*


*Our minds can sometimes freeze in summer.*

# 76. BLUR

**BLURRY THINGS ARE WAY CLEARER, UNUSUALLY.**

*Eyes blur, this time not by tears but sweat.*

# 77. TRAFFIC

*SUMMER THINGS RADIATE FROM AFAR.*

*Traffic. Crowd. Fuel.*

*Honk. Scream. Rule.*

# Chapter78

## *ONE DOES ANOTHER AND SO ON...*

*Fire can boil food.*

*Hunger can boil human.*

# 79. SWEET

*NOT MANY THINGS ARE BITTERSWEET.*

*Most things that smell sweet aren't sweet!*

# 80. COMPLIMENT

**_EVERYTHING IS COOLER THAN SUMMER._**


_Summer once told me that I'm cool._

# 81. MELT

*A HUMAN CAN NEVER CARE ANY LESS.*

*Couldn't care less about broken hearts*

*in this period of hearts*

*melting away!*

# 82. DILLY-DALLY

**DOING NOTHING WON'T MAKE THE TIME PASS ANY SOONER.**

*Dilly-dally for hours, but the day won't pass.*

*Dilly-dally for days, but the summer won't pass.*

# 83. DRIP

## *SOME TIMES WE'RE PROUD OF OURSELVES.*

*If autumn is fall, then I shall name summer drip.*

# 84. CLOUDY

**SOMETIMES, CLOUDY IS BETTER THAN CLEAR SKY.**

*Even for the over thinkers,*

*summer makes their mind cloudy.*

# 85. UP

*PEOPLE JUST SAY WITHOUT DOING.*

*People say aim high.*

*Meanwhile in summer,*

*we can't even look up.*

# 86. THIRST

*A HUMAN'S THIRST CAN NEVER BE QUENCHED.*

*Ice-cream, juices, water, and all the other*

*failed ideas of quenching thirst...*

# 87. LONG

*I wished to stay till evening.*

*But this summer long day just*

*won't let it happen.*

# 88. TIME

**BAD TIMES ARE SLOW TO DEPART.**


*Maybe time has it bad in summer, it takes so long to pass...*

# 89. BREATH

*WE JUST NEED A PLACE TO CALM DOWN.*

When we're out of breath,

finding shade doesn't matter.

# 90. BURN

*INTENTIONS MATTER.*

*One thing that burns can definitely sooth*

*other thing that burns.*

# 91. WALK

*WALK. JUST WALK AHEAD.*

*It's okay to simply walk with no aim.*

*It's okay to simply return with no motive.*

# 92. SAME

**SOME SCHEDULES NEVER CHANGE.**

*In this world where everything changes,*

*birds are always the same.*

# 93. EXHAUSTION

*MIND DOESN'T SWEAT.*


*When people say that you can't get exhausted*


*without doing anything, they're wrong.*

# 94. SHOWER

**NO ONE WILL LEAD ASTRAY IF THEY
KNOW WHAT'S BEST FOR THEM.**

*In the pursuit of shower, we return home faster*


*without any detours in summer.*

# 95. ICE-CREAM

*WE DON'T REALLY CARE MUCH ABOUT
ANYHTING THESE DAYS.*

*I don't really care about things that can't get*

*a hold of itself, like an ice-cream*

*an summer.*

# 96. SMART

**NO ONE HEARS A THING.**

*They said "how smart!" gracefully.*

*And then, "how stupid!" whispering right after.*

# 97. BLANKETS

*LETTING GO IS THE METHOD OF COMING BACK.*

*We must let go of people that are*

*hostile like the blankets.*

# 98. SWEATER

*WE'VE LEARNT TOO MUCH FROM NATURE.*

*Funny how nature teaches us to put away*

*things that are no longer needed—*

*Like sweaters.*

# 99. NATURE

*NATURE IS IRONIC!*

*Ironic how people become cool and*

*carefree in hot times!*

# 100. STONE

*WE ALL THINK WE'RE DIAMONDS WHEN WE'RE JUST STONES.*

*Learn from the stones to be who you are.*

*A diamond isn't precious until it's not found.*

# 101. INDIFFERENT

*BE UNIQUE SUGGESTS ONE TO BE
NORMAL.*


*Trying to be different is the most indifferent act.*

# 102. SHREWD

**WE SAY THINGS WHICH DOESN'T NEED TO BE SAID.**

*We're shrewd when not needy.*

# 103. COWARDS

*WE'RE ALL THE SAME.*

*No one is brave or coward.*

*We're all brave cowards.*

# 104. MIDDLE

*IN BETWEEN, WE FIND TROUBLE.*

*The beginning and ending is always the same.*

*Dusk and dawn.*

*Life and death.*

*The middle is the problem. The good. The bad.*

# 105. TRUTH

*NOTHIING IS HIDDEN.*

Truth can hide itself.

Lies can't.

Shade can hide itself.

Light can't.

# 106. DIFFERENCE

**INSIDE OR OUTSIDE, WE BELONG
SOMEWHERE.**

*It's all about the difference between just two steps.*

# 107. LATE AFTERNOON

*SOMETIMES URGES BECOME EMOTIONS.*


*We're hungry, thirsty and drowsy at the same time—*


*Late afternoons.*

# 108. GROWTH

*A WHILE LASTS WAY LONGER.*


*As the time passes, heat grows.*


*Here we kept thinking things might*


*get better after a while!*

# 109. TREES

## HOW YOU'RE TREATED DEPENDS ON YOU.

The hot breeze treats the trees same


way cool breeze did.

# 110. SOON

## *HUMANS JUST WANT THINGS TO REMAIN AS IT IS.*

*The sun shall set sooner.*

*The day shall end sooner.*

*We'll be where we were.*

*We'll stay how we were.*

# 111. VIOLET

## THINGS ASCEND AND DESCEND IN A FASHION.


Yellow. Less yellow.


Orange. More orange.


Blue. Purple. Violet. More violet.

# 112. WARNING

*IN OUR HEARTS WE KNOW, WE CAN BEAR THE HEAT.*


*Even a long summer day passes without any warning—*


*In a niche of time.*

# 113. EVERYTHING

*WE KNOW NOTHING ACTUALLY.*

*I don't know what's ahead.*

*But I know there's more heat.*

# 114. SAND

**OUR BODY IS STRONG AND FRAGILE.**

*We're all born from sand.*

*Our brain is silica.*

*Our heart is glass.*

# 115. STORM

**WE WILT BY EVERY PASSING SUMMER.**

*Summer is nothing for people.*

*We've faced enough storms.*

# 116. WAY

**IN THE END, NO COLOUR IS IMPORTANT.**

*Don't remind me of colours.*

*I'm still trying to find my way out of blue.*

# 117. AROMA

*THE PHASE BETWEEN ENDING AND BEGINNING IS HAUNTING.*

*The aroma of strong tea marks the*

*end of an afternoon—*

*Evening barges in.*

# 118. EVENING

**THE PHASE BETWEEN ENDING AND
BEGINNING IS HAUNTING.**

*Evening is a completely different aura.*

# Greatful

*I'm deeply, from the bottom of my heart, from the depths that echo,*

*greatful to each one who has reached the end. I hope this book has*

*made a place for itself in your hearts as well.*